MW00528765

Love,

Pastor Larry

PULLING DOWN STRONGHOLDS

◆ ◆ ◆

A Practical, Bible-Based Study on Spiritual Warfare

◆ ◆ ◆

PASTOR LARRY BRIGGS

©2020 by Larry Briggs

All rights reserved. No portion of this book may be reproduced, stored in a retrieval system, or transmitted in any form or by any means—electronic, mechanical, photocopy, recording, scanning, or other—except for brief quotations for review or citing purposes, without the prior written permission of the author.

All Bible verses quoted New King James Version Minister's Bible

Published by Argyle Fox Publishing, argylefoxpublishing.com

Publisher holds no responsibility for content of this work. Content is the sole responsibility of the author.

ISBN 978-1-953259-06-6 (Paperback)
ISBN 978-1-953259-07-3 (Ebook)

ARGYLE FOX
PUBLISHING

CONTENTS

PREFACE

9

STATEMENT OF PURPOSE

11

UNDERSTANDING SPIRITUAL WARFARE

13

IDENTIFYING THE ENEMY

15

THE BATTLEGROUNDS

25

THE WEAPONS OF OUR WARFARE

47

EPILOGUE:
LIVING VICTORIOUSLY

59

THE CHURCH'S DECLARATION

67

PREFACE

You and I are living in the most critical era the Church of Jesus Christ has ever faced. From the day of its birth on the day of Pentecost and throughout history, the Church has been under attack. We have a powerful and persistent enemy whose mission is clearly defined by Jesus in John 10:10: "The thief does not come except to steal, and to kill, and to destroy. I have come that they may have life, and that they may have it more abundantly."

Peter further describes this war in his first epistle. I Peter 5:8 exhorts us to

> "Be sober, be vigilant; because your adversary the devil walks about like a roaring lion, seeking whom he may devour. Resist him, steadfast in the faith, knowing that the same sufferings are experienced by your brotherhood in the world."

Although this war is not new, we need to be keenly aware that we are living in the last days. Hence why the intensity of our battle increases nearly every day. Satan, our adversary, knows his time is limited. As we will learn in this study, he is powerful, wise, and relentless in his attack on believers in Jesus Christ.

Satan's mission is to destroy the Church by rendering it weak and ineffective, thus preventing us from rescuing those under his influence, which is our most important mandate.

His plan to accomplish this is two-fold. He attacks us with outside forces and joins us, influencing us to destroy the Church from within. As we will note, Scripture is full of warnings referring to Satan's last-day effort, an effort that thankfully will fail.

My concern in this study is not the Church as a whole, but on you, the individual believer. How are you handling this battle on a personal level? Will you be an overcomer or like too many, will you be defeated? Note what the Apostle Paul wrote to Timothy, a young pastor.

"Now the Spirit expressly says that in latter times some will depart from the faith, giving heed to deceiving spirits and doctrines of demons, speaking lies in hypocrisy, having their own conscience seared with a hot iron, forbidding to marry, and commanding to abstain from foods which God created to be received with thanksgiving by those who believe and know the truth." (I Timothy 4:1–3)

In these critical hours in which we now live, it is imperative that the Church wake up and pray for eyes to see and ears to hear what the Spirit is saying to us. It is my sincere prayer that each believer who joins in this study will be personally equipped to identify and defeat our adversary, the devil.

Serving His servants,

Pastor Larry

STATEMENT OF PURPOSE

The Church is under attack. You and I are living in one of the most strategic periods of God's eternal plan for all ages. We are not here by chance nor coincidence, but by divine appointment. If we are going to fulfill our destiny given by our Heavenly Father, each one of us must intentionally cultivate an intimate and personal relationship with Jesus. We must submit to the lordship of Christ in every area of our lives, thus aborting Satan's attempts to weaken the Church and render it powerless and ineffective.

In Matthew 11:12, Jesus spoke concerning the age in which we now live. He said, "And from the days of John the Baptist until now the kingdom of Heaven suffers violence, and the violent take it by force." Jesus did not come to give birth to a pious, passive Church full of people who are content with occupying a pew on Sunday morning. His intent was to birth an aggressive Church that would not fear nor run from His enemy. A community of believers that would understand their authority in Christ and their commission to pull down strongholds and conqueror the gates of hell.

We have been empowered by the Holy Spirit to confront and conquer our enemy, identified by the Apostle Paul in Ephesians 6:12.

"For we do not wrestle against flesh and blood, but against principalities, against powers, against the rulers of the darkness of this age, against spiritual hosts of wickedness in heavenly places."

In his letter to the Corinthian church, Paul also teaches that we are not ignorant of Satan's devices: "Lest Satan should take advantage of us; for we are not ignorant of his devices." (II Corinthians 2:11)

My intent and purpose in writing this study is neither to glorify Satan nor give him undue attention. I believe that it is important for us, the Church, to be educated concerning the war we are engaged in and to know the plans and activities of our enemy.

You will find that the principles taught in this book are practical, balanced, and most importantly, Biblically sound. My sole purpose in preparing this study is to aid you in your battles by identifying the presence and plan of our enemy and equipping you as a soldier in the great army of our God.

"And you therefore, my son, be strong in the grace that is in Christ Jesus. And the things that you have heard from me among many witnesses, commit these to faithful men who will be able to teach others also. You therefore must endure hardship as a good soldier of Jesus Christ." (II Timothy 2:1–3)

UNDERSTANDING SPIRITUAL WARFARE

From creation until now, a spiritual war has been in process between our Heavenly Father and Lucifer, the fallen angel, and his cohorts. As stated previously, Jesus clearly defines this ongoing conflict and its participants.

"The thief does not come except to steal, and to kill, and to destroy. I have come that they may have life, and that they may have it more abundantly." (John 10:10)

In his Epistle, the Apostle Peter also speaks to this ongoing war between the Church and God's enemy. In I Peter 5:8, he writes, "Be sober, be vigilant; because your adversary the devil walks about like a roaring lion, seeking whom he may devour."

Scripture clearly teaches us that this war will continue until the second coming of Christ and the end of the world as we know it.

If you and I are to be the overcomers God planned for us to be, we must develop a Biblical understanding of this war and our participation in it.

In our study, we will focus on three major areas of this conflict.

First, we must understand the war by identifying our enemy and the battlegrounds upon which we are fighting.

Second, we will identify the weapons of our warfare and how to properly utilize each of them.

Third, we will close with an all-important addendum, a teaching on how to live victoriously in the freedom that Jesus has purchased for us.

IDENTIFYING THE ENEMY

To fully understand this war we must identify our enemy and the battleground upon which we fight. The Apostle Paul identifies our enemy as the god of this present world system.

In II Corinthians 4:3–4, he writes,

"But even if our gospel is veiled, it is veiled to those who are perishing, whose minds the god of this age has blinded, who do not believe, lest the light of the Gospel of the glory of Christ, who is the image of God, should shine on them."

Satan and his army are active in our world today, and his influence can be seen in our nation and throughout the world. Time doesn't permit us to fully explore this phenomenon, but we must be aware of Satan's presence among us. Just because you can't see him doesn't mean he does not exist.

The Apostle Paul explains this in his writing to the Colossian church.

PULLING DOWN STRONGHOLDS

"For by him [Jesus] all things were created that are in Heaven and that are on earth, visible and invisible, whether thrones or dominions or principalities or powers. All things were created through Him and for Him." (Colossians 1:16)

It is heartbreaking and sad to admit, but America the beautiful is being torn apart by these demonic forces. The evil we are witnessing cannot be solved by political genius, military power, or governmental leadership. Many of our elected officials are good people who are blinded by these demonic spirits. Under their influence, these officials are making critical decisions that will result in the total destruction of our nation. The spirit of the Antichrist is clearly at work and this battle cannot be won by physical means.

It is time for the Church to wake up and be the Church that Jesus intended us to be. Spiritual forces can only be defeated by Spirit-filled believers rising up, taking a stand, and confronting these evil forces in the might and power of the Holy Spirit. As we seek Him and fully surrender to His lordship, He will use us to drive out and conquer the enemy of our souls. As Paul wrote to the Corinthians, if we are listening, the Holy Spirit will reveal the enemy's plan and activities to us.

Satan's five-fold mission is defined for us in Ezekiel 28:11–19 and Isaiah 14:12–19. Carefully read these Old Testament Scriptures and you will see Satan's goals.

Goal 1: Satan stated, "I will ascend into Heaven." His desire is to occupy the place of God in the world and in our personal lives.

Goal 2: He goes on to declare, "I will exalt my throne above the stars of God." Satan wants total control of our lives and world.

Goal 3: Next, he openly states, "I will sit on the Mount of Congregation." In Scripture, the Mount of Congregation is the place for worship. Satan is insistent on getting us to worship him. He does this through the influence of social media, music, and entertainment. Whatever gets the majority of our focus in life naturally becomes our idol (god). We need to be very sensitive to the conviction of the Holy Spirit in our lives. He will prevent us from falling into this trap.

Goal 4: Satan declares his intent to "ascend above the heights of the clouds." He wants to take God's glory for himself.

Goal 5: Finally, he boldly declares, "I will be like the Most High." His mission is to become the supreme ruler both in our personal lives and the world.

It is interesting to note that when the Church was born on the day of Pentecost in Acts 2, God equipped us with a five-fold ministry (Ephesians 4:11–12) to counterattack Satan's five-fold mission and his evil forces:

> *"And He Himself gave some apostles, some prophets, some evangelists, and some pastors and teachers for the equipping of the saints for the work of ministry, for the edifying of the body of Christ."*

Each of these offices was appointed to equip us to be a strong and aggressive Church, standing against the schemes of our enemy.

Ministry 1: Apostles were appointed to serve as overseers of several churches or ministries within a specific region. Their primary focus was on providing guidance and counsel to the local pastors and leaders.

Ministry 2: Prophets were appointed to provide spiritual exhortation and understanding, which reflected the reality of the present and future, to the Church as a whole. They were mostly traveling ministers sent out and approved by the Apostolic leadership.

Ministry 3: Evangelists were appointed by the leaders of the local congregations. Their focus was on preaching the Gospel and bringing people to the knowledge of salvation through the sacrifice of Jesus on the cross. They traveled from church to church, bringing inspiration, encouragement, and correction.

Ministry 4: Pastors were ordained to oversee local congregations. Their ministry involved preaching, teaching, discipling, and protecting the fellowship of believers to whom they were assigned.

Ministry 5: Teachers were appointed by pastors to assist in bringing spiritual exhortation and instruction in the Word to their followers.

Each of these offices was designed individually by God to function together as a team in order to provide ministry to the Church as a whole.

God never intended for the Church to be led by a single individual. His plan was to use a team of leaders whose sole motivation was to fulfill the call of God on their lives. To successfully propagate the Gospel, every local church needs each of these offices functioning together simultaneously.

When the Church functions in the power of the Holy Spirit, Satan has no hope of accomplishing his mission. Together as a team, we are empowered to bring down strongholds and to bring every thought and imagination to the obedience of Christ (II Corinthians 10:3–6).

Satan was cast out of Heaven because of his rebellion. We were created to glorify God by defeating the enemy in our daily lives. However, when Adam and Eve disobeyed God, Satan gained control over the earth. He remains a powerful influence even until today. This is what Paul meant when he referred to him as the "god of this present world."

But Jesus, the second Adam, conquered Satan at the cross. When Jesus rose from the grave, He was given the keys of authority, the keys of life and death. After His resurrection on the day of Pentecost, Jesus turned over those keys to the Church— that's us!. By the indwelling of the Holy Spirit, He gave us authority in His name over the power of the enemy.

> *"Then the seventy returned with joy, saying, 'Lord, even the demons are subject to us in your name.' And He said to them, 'I saw Satan fall like lightning from Heaven. Behold, I give you the authority to trample on serpents and scorpions, and over all the power of the enemy, and nothing shall by any means hurt you.'" (Luke 10:17–19)*

In his short Epistle, Jude gives clear, practical insight concerning our enemy and how he works. I encourage you to pause and prayerfully read his Epistle. Then note that in verses 1–7, Satan's main cause—his mission—is to bring **deception** into the Church.

In these opening verses, Jude addresses the urgency of this issue and changes direction in subject matter. He then informs us of how Satan enters into our fellowship as worms in a slow, methodical process. In verses 5–7, Jude warns of the end results if we allow this to happen: that there will be disunity among believers that results in distraction and destruction. Unfortunately, this is prevalent in many congregations today.

Then in verses 8–11, Jude exposes our enemy's conduct. He appears as self-proclaimed prophets who exhibit false spiritual gifts and dreams. They openly defy authority—especially spiritual authority, and they consistently speak evil against God's appointed spiritual leaders. By doing this, they hope to create an environment of doubt and disunity within the Church. These false prophets can easily be detected by their immoral conduct and greed.

Jude then unveils Satan's character in verses 10–11. We can expect these same characteristics to be evident in those under his influence. Those who focus on the flesh and earthly things more than the spiritual are under the deceptive influence of our enemy. Jude identifies three dominant spirits that will be at work in the last days.

Sadly, they are also present in the Church.

1. The spirit of Cain, which is revealed through a propensity for violence.

2. The spirit of Balaam, an overpowering desire (lust) for self-gratification. Under the influence of this spirit, the Church will overemphasize money and prosperity. There will be a trend to merchandize the Gospel and measure success by financial profit rather than how many lives are saved and rescued from the darkness of Satan's grip.

3. The horrific spirit of Korah. This spirit will infiltrate the Church with spiritual rebellion against our appointed spiritual leaders. It will manifest itself through those who exhibit discontent against pastors and Church leaders. Its purpose is to create disunity and dysfunction in order to render the Church weak and ineffective in the local community where it has been planted.

As an interesting sidebar, consider what John the Revelator saw and recorded in Revelation 16:13.

"And I saw three unclean spirits like frogs coming out of the mouth of the dragon, and out of the mouth of the beast, and out of the mouth of the false prophet."

Scripture clearly warns us to beware Satan's presence and activity within the last-day Church. Remember, we are not ignorant of his devices, and we have been made more than conquerors!

In the next four verses, 12–16, Jude's focus is on the consequences of being unaware of the enemy's presence and the havoc he can create in the Church and world. Jude states that there will be spots (reefs) in your fellowship that can result in shipwreck. Reefs are underwater and are not easily seen by the natural eye.

Secondly, Jude warns that these spirits are like clouds without water. They look good but are useless. He then continues, describing these spirits as trees without fruit. They take up space but are non-productive.

Remember as we consider the consequences Jude describes, he is referring to frogs in our fellowship. People under Satan's influence have been assigned to the Church to create confusion and destruction. Let me encourage you not to become paranoid and look at everyone as frogs. Seek the gift of discernment and allow the Holy Spirit to open our spiritual eyes.

Jude continues by describing these false prophets and spirits as wild waves that dredge up garbage onto the shore. They are like wandering stars—unstable, uncommitted, and constantly moving from place to place.

Finally, Jude closes this section by warning us that these frogs, these wild waves, these wandering stars are easily recognizable. They are those people who constantly grumble and complain, sowing discord and disunity within the Church. They should be approached as brothers and sisters in Christ and exhorted to repent and follow Christ. If they refuse to do so, we must ignore them and have no fellowship with them.

Jude closes his epistle with an exhortation to each believer. In verses 17–23, he explains our calling. We are to cultivate unity in the Spirit within the Church (17–19), be faithful through persistent prayer and the cultivation of strong, godly relationships (20), and live holy lives (21) in order to maintain our victory. He also emphasizes the importance of showing mercy (22) and concludes with encouragement to focus on evangelism—rescuing others from Satan's grip (23).

Jude's message is that God has empowered us with His Holy Spirit to identify and conquer Satan and his cohorts, in the Church and in our personal lives. God's plan is for us to move forward as **VICTORS** not **VICTIMS**.

Another important discourse on this issue is given by the physician Luke, who reveals the reality of this war and our enemy in the eleventh chapter of his gospel. This is not fantasy, science fiction, or some mystical phenomenon glamorized by Hollywood. This is reality. It is a horrific war between two kingdoms diabolically opposed to each other.

Luke describes our enemy as Beelzebub, the prince of darkness. He is a ruler who commands an organized army of strong, well-armed demons. His motive is total destruction and possession. His methods are deception, intimidation, and temptation. His main weapons are spiritual ignorance and carnal living.

We cannot ignore our enemy's presence among us. We must "pray without ceasing," stay alert and strong, and always be "instant in season and out," allowing the Holy Spirit to renew our minds daily.

Understanding the war by identifying the enemy from a Biblical perspective enables us to fight as good soldiers of Jesus Christ. Equally important is learning where we do battle. Knowing the battleground and mapping the landscape enables us to be better prepared when the enemy strikes.

"For this cause we also, since the day we heard it, do not cease to pray for you, and to desire that you might be filled with the knowledge of His will in all wisdom and spiritual understanding; that you might walk worthy of our Lord unto all pleasing, being fruitful in every good work, and increasing in the knowledge of God; strengthened with all might, according to His glorious power, unto all patience and longsuffering with joyfulness; giving thanks unto the Father, which hath made us meet to be partakers of the inheritance of the saints in light: Who hath delivered us from the power of darkness, and hath translated us into the kingdom of his dear son: In whom we have redemption through His blood, even the forgiveness of sins." (Colossians 1:3–14)

THE BATTLEGROUNDS

To defeat the enemy, we must educate ourselves on the battlefields upon which we fight. In these critical times in which we live, the Church has a great opportunity to put the devil in his rightful place while rescuing those under his influence and bondage.

The Apostle Paul wrote a bold and powerful statement in reference to our battlegrounds in II Corinthians 4:7–12.

"But we have this treasure [knowledge of the glory of God] in earthen vessels, that the excellence of the power may be of God and not of us. We are hard pressed on every side, yet not crushed; we are perplexed, but not in despair; persecuted, but not forsaken; struck down, but not destroyed. Always carrying about in the body the dying of the Lord Jesus, that the life of Jesus also may be manifested in our body. For we who live are [always] delivered to death for Jesus's sake, that the life of Jesus also may be manifested in our mortal flesh. So then death is working in us, but life in you."

PULLING DOWN STRONGHOLDS

A close examination of this text reveals the intensity of our battles, where they are fought, and the purpose of them. While painful and difficult, we are sent into battle to help us die to our flesh so that we might live in God's Spirit.

More often than not, the first and most effective place Satan attacks us is in our minds. He knows if he can control our thinking he can control us. That is why we find so many Scriptures referencing our need to allow the Holy Spirit to renew our minds on a daily basis. Note these primary texts. Each is a powerful weapon against the schemes of the devil.

"For those who live according to the flesh set their minds on the things of the flesh, but those who live according to the Spirit, the things of the Spirit. For to be carnally minded is death, but to be spiritually minded is life and peace." (Romans 8:5–6)

"I beseech you, therefore brethren, by the mercies of God, that you present your bodies a [living] sacrifice, holy acceptable unto God, which is your reasonable service. And do not be conformed to this world, but be transformed by the renewing of your mind, that you may prove what is that good and acceptable and perfect will of God." (Romans 12:1–2)

"For though we walk in the flesh, we do not war according to the flesh. For the weapons of our warfare are not carnal but mighty in God for pulling down strongholds, casting down arguments and every high thing that exalts itself against the knowledge of God, bringing every thought into captivity to the obedience of Christ, and being ready

to punish all disobedience [when your obedience is fulfilled]." (II Corinthians 10:3–6)

"Let this mind be in you which was also in Christ Jesus." (Philippians 2:5)

"Finally brethren, whatever things are true, whatever things are noble, whatever things are just, whatever things are pure, whatever things are lovely, whatever things are of good report, if there is any virtue and if there is anything praiseworthy; meditate on these things." (Philippians 4:8)

"For God has not given us a spirit of fear, but of power and of love and of a sound mind." (II Timothy 1:7)

There are two principles involved in the concept of "renewing our minds" that we need to discuss. Both are found in the above Scriptures.

Principle 1: It is a ministry of the Holy Spirit that strengthens us by renewing our minds. He has absolute power over our enemy. He alone can cancel every demonic thought placed in our minds, and He alone can fill us with the power of God and create in us the very mind of Christ (Philippians 2:5).

Principle 2: Although the Holy Spirit is omnipotent, He can only do what we allow Him to do in our lives. We desperately need to understand that we are partners with the Holy

Spirit. If we do our part, He is faithful to do His. Our part is to daily submit to the Lordship of Jesus Christ and give Him total control over every area of our lives.

The Bible clearly teaches that our greatest defense against the devil is living in total obedience to the Word and will of God. By emptying ourselves of every carnal desire and seeking first the kingdom of God, we can be filled with His Spirit and power. This is what the Apostle Paul teaches in Galatians 5. Walking in the Spirit enables us to overcome the enemy and every thought he tries to place in our minds. We can only do this by the grace and power of God.

> *"I say then: Walk in the Spirit, and you shall not fulfill the lust of the flesh. For the flesh lusts against the Spirit, and the Spirit against the flesh; and these are contrary to one another, so that you do not the things that you wish. But if you are led by the Spirit, you are not under the law." (Galatians 5:16—8)*

On the mind's battleground, there are three main weapons Satan utilizes: deception, intimidation, and temptation.

Deception. Let me help you understand a basic truth of spiritual war. In every life situation we are influenced by three spirits. Most importantly as Christians, the Holy Spirit is present to provide wisdom and guidance into the will of God. At the same time, demonic spirits are trying to direct us into confusion and chaos. Equally powerful is the spirit of man, experienced through our own thoughts and feelings.

This is one of the main reasons Paul teaches us to "pray without ceasing" (I Thessalonians 5:16). He is not suggesting that we lock ourselves in a room and pray twenty-four hours a day. He speaks of the Biblical concept of prayer and living in the Spirit.

We should never be in a place mentally or physically that the Holy Spirit is hindered from speaking to us. We must intentionally abstain from the very presence of evil by being cautious of what we listen to, what we read, and the places of entertainment we visit. This empowers us to maintain sensitivity to God's presence and live in such a manner that He can always direct and convict us.

The Spirit is ever-present, keeping us on the right path and preventing us from falling into the enemy's traps. In these days of intense battle, we need to earnestly seek the gift of discernment from the Holy Spirit so that we don't fall victim to our enemy's schemes and deception. The Spirit of Truth will always guide us into truth, and the truth will keep us free.

Intimidation. Intimidation gives birth to fear, and fear—if allowed—will destroy our faith. Remind yourself what Paul taught the young pastor Timothy: "God has not given us a spirit of fear but of love, power, and a sound mind."

Intimidation is a direct attack on our minds. To conquer this horrific spirit we need to fill our minds with the Word of God and daily remind ourselves who we are in Christ Jesus. He is our champion who has already won the war for us.

At the time of this writing, our world and nation are under attack from the horrible COVID-19 virus. I believe this virus is demonic, sent to paralyze the Church. Of course, we must use wisdom and follow guidelines to protect ourselves and others, but we cannot surrender to fear and intimidation.

It is a bad decision by our political leaders to shut down churches, while liquor stores continue to operate. It is poor leadership to limit attendance at worship services, while at the same time allowing protests and rioting to take place in our public squares.

This is a spiritual battle, and we need to see it for what it is. Now more than ever, the Church needs to wake up, stand up, and be the Church He birthed us to be. We are warriors, not wimps, and we should refuse to live in fear of anything the enemy produces. Just remember, we are not fighting flesh and blood (politicians and government leaders). We are fighting principalities and powers in heavenly realms. As such, our victory will never come through the genius of man but only through prayer and fasting.

Temptation. Note the warning of James 1:12–15:

"Blessed is the man who endures temptation; for when he has been approved, he will receive the crown of life which the Lord has promised to those who love Him. Let no one say when he is tempted, 'I am tempted by God'; for God cannot be tempted by evil, nor does He Himself tempt anyone. But each one is tempted when he is drawn away by his own desires and enticed. Then when desire has conceived, it gives birth to sin; and sin, when it is full-grown, brings forth death."

Temptation is a battle we all face on a daily basis. We cannot escape it, but we can conquer it. It is a battle between our flesh and the Spirit. Note an important insight James gives us in this battle. He speaks of the crown of life to be given to those who overcome temptation, that it will be rewarded to those "who love God." We overcome temptation by loving God more than the thing Satan tempts us with.

This is why I am so passionate about teaching believers the importance of cultivating an intimate and personal relationship with Jesus. The more we love him, the less we love the things of this world!

In my last book, *The Secret Place: 7 Meditations for the Last-Day Church*, I teach the importance of this and how to obtain it. Sin is a matter of the heart. Too many of God's people are losing this battle, not because they are weak but because they don't understand this all-important spiritual truth.

Scripture warns us that many in the last days will fall away because their hearts will grow cold to the things of God, causing them to love themselves more than God. These people exchange the truth of God and believe the lies of the enemy (Romans 1). Unfortunately, many have fallen into this trap. They justify sin and believe they can live contrary to the teaching of God's Word because it feels good and is culturally acceptable.

Greed and sexual sin is rampant in the Church, and many pastors are hesitant to speak against it. If we are to win this war and rescue those caught in Satan's traps, we must speak out boldly, without apology.

The truth is that God loves you, and I do too. In fact, I love you too much to turn a blind eye to this wildly spreading cancer in our faith communities.

Just because our culture accepts something does not make it right in the eyes of God. Culture changes and it has changed the Church in many ways. But we serve a God who never changes. As Hebrews 13:8 lays out so beautifully: "Jesus Christ is the same yesterday, today, and forever." And God clearly states in His Word to us,

"Do not love the world or the things in the world. If anyone [you] loves the world, the love of the Father is not in him. For all that is in the world: the lust of the flesh, the lust of the eyes, and the pride of

life, is not of the Father but is of the world. And the world is passing away, and the lust of it; but he who does the will of God abides forever." (I John 2:15–17)

I don't understand how any Christian can ignore this truth and decisively live in a manner contrary to God's Word. But, as Scripture warns, these are the last days, and some will heed seducing spirits and doctrines of demons. I pray fervently that you are not one of them.

God, through Jesus Christ, has provided victory over the enemy and all of his weapons. He has made us more than conquerors, and we are without excuse. On this battleground of the mind, turn your eyes upon Jesus, the author and finisher of your faith (Hebrews 12:2) and live in the victory He has provided.

"He who has an ear, let him hear what the Spirit says to the churches. To him who overcomes I will give some of the hidden manna to eat. And I will give him a white stone, and on the stone a new name written which no one knows except him who receives it." (Revelation 2:17)

Another battleground upon which Satan is focused is the home and family. No local church can be stronger than the families who attend it. The devil knows this and has unleashed an all-out attack on our homes. Many social problems we face today find their roots in the demise of the family unit and home as God originally planned. Many children are born out of wedlock and are raised by struggling single moms, grandparents, or foster families.

Without the structure and support of both a father and mother, many children today are left to discover important life issues on their own. Or, even worse, through others who prey on them and use them for sordid purposes.

As a result, we now have a generation of young people who don't know right from wrong. This is Satan's plan! And as hard as it is to admit, he is accomplishing his mission. But thank God, the Church is rising to the task, and thousands of young people across our nation are turning to Jesus through evangelistic efforts.

This is an ongoing battle, and we desperately need to re-focus on our families and homes. Every father is called by God to be the priest and spiritual leader of his family, and many are abdicating their responsibility. Any male can have sex and impregnate a woman, but it takes a real man to be a faithful and committed husband and father.

Men, we are under attack. It is high time we stand up to our enemy and bring the protection and favor of God into our homes.

In this family and home battle, I want to share four important areas we need to strengthen. The Holy Spirit is revealing the strategy of the enemy so we can build an effective defense against him. God created the family before He built His Church, so the family must be a priority for us.

The first battlefront is in personal contentment. Paul states in I Timothy 6:6 that "Godliness with contentment is great gain." One of Satan's main weapons is temptation, and many families have been damaged or destroyed by discontentment.

It is dangerous to always want more, to always want something new, to never be satisfied with what Father has

33

provided. Because no person or thing can make us happy. We must discover our happiness in life can only be found in a personal relationship with our Lord Jesus Christ.

Our rule in life should be grounded in Paul's counsel in Philippians 4:11–13. There, Paul stresses the same principle and truth he spoke to Timothy—that contentment with godly living is great gain. We strengthen our relationships with each other by putting God first in every area of our lives.

We literally close the door of our homes and families to Satan by putting Jesus on the throne of our hearts and allowing Him to reign as our Saviour and Lord. Our key to victory in this critical area of our lives is revealed in Philippians 4:11–13.

"Not that I speak in regard to need, for I have learned in whatever state I am, to be content. I know how to be abased, and I know how to abound. Everywhere and in all things I have learned both to be full and to be hungry, both to abound and to suffer need. I can do all things through Christ who strengthens me."

Another critical area we need to focus on within our families is intimacy. This is an area Satan focuses on, and our best defense against him is to build our relationships as God planned them. Marital infidelity is a powerful weapon the enemy uses to destroy lives and demolish the family unit. There is a sensuous (sexual) spirit running rampant in our world and the Church. The same spirit responsible for the fall of the Roman empire, it will destroy us if left unchecked. It can only be defeated by the consistent use of our spiritual weapons.

I learned years ago that the most effective weapon against the enemy is a firm commitment to live according to the Word of God, not by my feelings. To that end, I adopted a spiritual principle that always works in this battle against the flesh. That principle? To intentionally do the opposite of what the enemy tries to influence me to do.

Let me give an example. When I came up in the ministry, a prevailing Church philosophy was that to keep a pastor humble, he must remain in poverty. Thank God those days are in the past! There have been many times when Jane and I suffered financially and literally had to trust God for our daily needs. Often during such times, the enemy would try to influence me to not tithe. He wanted me to believe that God would understand. I needed the money, after all. And I must confess that I listened in a few cases. The results were disastrous.

Thanks to those specific cases, I learned to do the exact opposite of whatever the enemy encouraged me to do. Not only do I give my tithe, but I increase it. I give an offering to our great God, and it is a joy to do so.

At Destination Church, where I currently serve, we take one special offering each year during the Christmas season. Everything that comes in for that offering is given to other ministries, missions, and community needs.

Last year as the time of this offering approached, Jane and I prayed for direction. While the amount that the Holy Spirit deposited into my thinking would not have been a sacrifice, it was a stretch. We live on a tight budget, so we have to be wise with our spending. Of course, the enemy used this knowledge against me. He tried convincing me to give less. But years of training helped me see Satan's lies for what they were. So I followed the principle. I gave more than the Spirit led me to give and double what the enemy suggested.

This offering to God required disciplined living and left less for Christmas giving. Nonetheless, we gave as planned. While leaving the service that Sunday morning, an elderly African American sister handed me a Christmas card with a kind hug.

After lunch, I opened the card, expecting a nice Christmas greeting from this precious sister who lives a very simple life. The card and greeting were beautiful, but something else really got my attention. Inside was a check for ten times the amount we had given. Our ten grandchildren reaped the harvest that Christmas, and we learned again what the Prophets taught is true: God values obedience over sacrifice.

However, God will not always reward with financial blessings as He did with us here. Even if we had not received this gift, the enemy was defeated. Father has many ways of providing for us and gladly does so as we learn obedience in this battle.

When it comes to this battle against the flesh, we must be intentional. Cultivating good relationships within the family is critically important, and it doesn't happen automatically. It requires time and effort.

We've all heard the saying, "The family that prays together stays together," and it's true. Also true is the fact that "The family that *plays* together stays together." Intimacy (closeness) is not only important between a husband and wife. It is equally important between parents and children and siblings.

The family unit was created to provide for our most basic needs—physically, emotionally, and spiritually. If we are not in a right relationship with God, we cannot be in a right relationship with each other. Scripture also teaches the opposite truth. If we don't foster right relationships with each other, we can't have a right relationship with our Heavenly Father.

Prayerfully consider the cross—God's provision for our salvation, healing, and freedom. It is both horizontal and vertical, symbolizing the importance of all our relationships: vertical with God and horizontally with each other.

To increase the intimacy of our relationships, we must establish boundaries by setting our priorities.

As a pastor, I learned early on that time is a valuable treasure. Schedules, people, and genuine needs are always demanding my attention. However, one of the most important things the Lord taught me was to prioritize my family. I was privileged to be the father of three boys and the husband of a great wife. What profit would it be if I won the whole world to Christ and lost even one of them?

Your family is your greatest treasure in life and deserves to be on the top of your priorities. God is not jealous of the time you spend with your family if you intentionally put Him first and don't allow them or anything else to take His place on the throne of your heart. They make up your most important, most immediate ministry. Prayerfully consider this critical area of your life and don't give place to the devil in your home. Shut the door to the enemy by making your family your most valued treasure and priority. Your rewards will be unmeasurable.

Communication is another critical focus in our homes that is a target of Satan. All couples and families struggle with this issue.

In our counseling ministry, Jane and I find communication to be one of the most common problems in all sorts of relationships. Because it involves two or more individuals, communication is complex. Communication combines different personalities, different past experiences, and different perspectives with emotion. If not handled carefully, the end results can be disastrous.

Clear communication is founded on two principles. All

parties must have the opportunity to clearly state their personal perspective and feelings, and all participants must intentionally listen to the other. Remember, everything you hear is filtered through your past experiences and feelings. Fail to understand this and mismanage a conversation, and you will likely misinterpret what is said to you.

Therefore, we must discipline ourselves to listen to others. It is an ongoing battle, and the enemy constantly works to create confusion and offense. I don't know that this struggle ever ends or that we can master this issue. Jane and I have ministered to couples who have been married for fifty years or more who still struggle with communication. But that is no reason to give up.

Want stronger, clearer communication? Focus on the one you're talking with rather than your own feelings and perspective. When you mess up, be humble, ask forgiveness, and walk in the Biblical teaching that encourages you to consider others greater than yourself. Utilize the spiritual principle previously discussed: *Do the exact opposite of what the enemy is trying to influence you to do.*

Note the exhortation of the Apostle James to the Church: "Confess your trespasses to one another, and pray for one another, that you may be healed. The effective, fervent prayer of a righteous man avails much." (James 5:16)

We will sometimes fail at communication, but if we maintain a right spirit within ourselves, we can make it right.

Early in my ministry, a respected and dearly loved mentor taught me a truth that has served me well. That truth? Relationships are valuable, and sometimes it's better to lose so others can win. In the end, such humility will help you be the winner.

Don't allow discouragement to overwhelm you in this

battle. When you fail, learn from your mistakes and determine to improve your listening and communication skills. I personally believe this is especially true in today's climate of political correctness and the newly developed "cancel culture."

Everyone deserves to be heard and understood, and we must learn to do that for others, even if we disagree with them. In Christ we can learn to disagree, agreeably. We aren't required to agree with every idea we hear. The mandate from our Father is to do all things in love. That includes loving others well enough to listen to what they have to say.

Make prayer a priority in your daily life. As you learn to listen to the Holy Spirit, He will help you better understand others. We may not view everything in life with spiritual eyes, but we should. Our Father watches over us and through His Spirit, He is with us in every situation. Let's learn to see Him as He works!

Closely related to this is the spirit of contention. Frequently birthed when communicating, contention can take root in your home if you're not on guard. It is Satan's goal to keep you upset and frustrated as much as possible. A great weapon to ward off this nagging spirit is found in Paul's exhortation in Romans 12:17–21.

"Repay no one evil for evil. Have regard for good things in the sight of all men. If it is possible, as much as depends on you, live peaceably with all men. Beloved, do not avenge yourselves, but rather give place to wrath; for it is written, 'Vengeance is mine, I will repay,' says the Lord. Therefore, 'If your enemy is hungry, feed him; if he is thirsty, give him a drink; for in so doing you will heap coals of fire on his head.' Do not be overcome by evil, but overcome evil with good."

Pulling Down Strongholds

The Apostle Paul knew the effectiveness of doing the opposite of what the devil tries to influence you to do. In fact, Paul was the author of that principle. And nowhere is it more applicable than the home and family.

If we permit our enemy to deposit a spirit of contention within our homes, we will see his destructive plans fulfilled. As Paul wrote, "Give no place to the devil." (Ephesians 4:27) We must constantly be on guard against his schemes and be aware that we are not fighting flesh and blood (each other), but Satan and his army.

The end result of all contention is division, and Jesus clearly taught that a house divided against itself cannot stand. To maintain peace in our homes we must intentionally foster an attitude of humility birthed out of love for one another. This requires daily attention and effort.

If we commit ourselves to live according to the principles of God's Word, no weapon or scheme of the enemy against us will be successful. Let me state it again, our best defense against the enemy is living a life of obedience unto God.

Life is all about relationships. Good relationships must be cultivated and carefully maintained. Jane and I recently celebrated our forty-ninth anniversary, and I confess it has not all been easy. But looking back, I can tell you that the time and effort we invested into each other reaped far better rewards than any sacrifices we made.

At Destination Church, where we serve under the leadership of our son, Bryan, we close every service stating, "The best is yet to come." We are a living testimony to the truth of that popular statement. So when the ugly spirit of contention tries to invade your hearts and home, neither panic nor submit to it, but as James taught in James 4:7, "Therefore submit to

God. Resist the devil and he will flee from you."

Another important battlefront within the home that needs exposure is the battle against the spirit of materialism. This spirit works in close proximity with the previously mentioned issues of contentment and contention.

Social sciences teach us that the two most powerful contributors to divorce and the demise of the family unit are sexual issues and financial problems. Many families, even in the Church, live under the influence of the spirit of materialism. The end result is found in the reality of many families that live beyond their financial means, abusing credit and putting themselves in a financial hole with no hope of escape.

The spirit of materialism influences us to never be satisfied (content) with what we have. We always want a bigger house, a newer car, the newest technologies, and the most popular clothes. It convinces us that using a credit card is easy and convenient. So we use that card to feed our hunger for instant gratification. We justify outlandish spending and lifestyles by convincing ourselves that we deserve the best.

But the best is not always having more stuff. In Scripture we are taught to live in moderation, content with the physical provisions of God, and hungering and thirsting after Jesus and righteousness.

The lust of the flesh is a real battle that most don't know exists. Instead, we just follow our whims, not realizing we've confused our wants with our needs. We need to take a serious look at the fact that we don't need most of what we think we need. Remember, there is a big difference between a need and a want (desire).

Self-discipline is not easy, but it is necessary if we are to gain victory over the flesh and all of its desires. And as a believer in Christ, you don't have to rely on your own will power. The same Spirit that raised Jesus from the dead is in you! Do you not think the Spirit is powerful enough to help curb your hunger for more things? He is! You can become more self-controlled. Note that self-control is one of the nine fruits of the Spirit listed by Paul in Galatians 5. In submitting to the lordship of Christ, He fills us with His Spirit and produces fruit that will glorify Him and defeat the devil.

Falling prey to materialism creates stress, anxiety, and unnecessary family problems. It robs us of the peace of God and fractures our relationships.

Fortunately for the Church today, there are vast resources for financial management and counseling. Take advantage of these educational materials and make a serious commitment to adopt a lifestyle that pleases our Heavenly Father.

Scripture teaches us to live in moderation and to seek first the kingdom of God. Determining to live according to the principles of God's Word will bring us the peace of God and His provisions.

> "Therefore do not worry, saying, 'What shall we eat?' or 'What shall we drink?' or 'What shall we wear?' for after all these things the Gentiles seek. For your Heavenly Father knows that you need all these things. But seek [first] the kingdom of God and His righteousness, and all these things will be added to you. Therefore do not worry about tomorrow, for tomorrow will worry about its own things. Sufficient for today is its own trouble." (Matthew 6: 31–34)

Jesus is not suggesting that we not plan and prepare for the future. Rather, he encourages us to live disciplined lives and trust Him to provide whatever material things we need.

Satan's main purpose in influencing us to surrender to the god of materialism is two-fold. First, to create stress, division, and destruction in the home. Second, to put us in such financial chaos and restraint that we are unable to tithe and give offerings to support God's work and ministries in the world.

When we put God first in all areas of our lives, including our finances, He will bless us beyond our imagination. This allows us to live with the same confidence that Paul expressed in Philippians 4:19: "And my God shall supply all your needs according to his riches in glory by Christ Jesus." God desires to bless us more than we want to be blessed. When we keep Him on the throne of our lives, every need will be met and we will be equipped to defeat the enemy on this critical battlefront.

His provision will not always come in financial blessings but as He promised, He will always provide what we need. If you do not have it, you do not need it to live a life pleasing to our God. Giving Him total control brings peace and security to our lives.

As we are learning, our enemy is diversified, and he attacks us in all areas of our lives. There are many battlegrounds upon which we must stand against his schemes. Before we turn our attention to the powerful weapons provided to us by our Heavenly Father for this battle, let's consider one more critical battleground. **That battleground is the Church.**

As previously stated, the Church is under attack. In Ephesians, the Apostle Paul had a lot to say about the Church. He describes the Church as the bride, body, and building of Christ (Ephesians 2:20–22). Each describes a specific purpose and function we have in this present world.

We are the Church, and we need to find our individual place

and function in it. If Satan can distract and discourage us, he can prevent the Church from being what Father birthed it to be. As God's body, voice, and instruments, we were created to reach a dying world.

(Note: I don't have space to dig into this here, but I suggest you study Paul's writing to the Corinthian Church. There you will discover that each one of us are a critical part of God's plan and family.)

We each have a place in our Father's house and an important role to perform. That is one reason Satan is so persistent in attacking us individually. He wants to distract you and me from our purpose in life, to prevent us from taking our place in the body of Christ. If he succeeds in this, the devil can keep the Church from its mission.

Satan's main weapons on this battlefront are deception, disunity, and distraction. We defeat him by surrendering to the lordship of Christ and fulfilling our personal responsibility as believers. (Prayerfully reread Romans 12:1–2.) As Paul instructs in Ephesians 6, if we put on the whole armor of God, we will be equipped to stand against any attack of the enemy. Only then will the Church be empowered to move forward as intended, crash the gates of hell, and rescue those taken into bondage by the enemy.

I believe the Church is Satan's main focus today. Therefore, we need to be sensitive to the Holy Spirit and allow Him to lead us in mounting a defense against the devil. And don't think you're not needed in this battle. This requires all hands on deck. You are an important part of Christ's bride, body, and building. We need each other in order to win this war. So please don't neglect the church by allowing the enemy to prevent you from taking your place.

There is power in unity and together, we stand.

I'll close this section with the exhortation of Paul in Romans 12:3–8.

"For I say, through the grace given to me, to everyone who is among you, not to think of himself more highly than he ought to think, but to think soberly, as God has dealt to each one a measure of faith. For as we have many members in one body, but all the members do not have the same function, so we, being many, are one body in Christ, and individually members of one another. Having then gifts differing according to the grace that is given to us, let us use them: if prophecy, let us prophecy in proportion to our faith; or ministry, let us use it in our ministering; he who teaches, in teaching; he who exhorts, in exhortation; he who gives, with liberality; he who leads, with diligence; he who shows mercy, with cheerfulness."

THE WEAPONS OF OUR WARFARE

In his letters to the church in Corinth, the Apostle Paul addresses spiritual warfare and our need to understand all of its ramifications. He specifically notes the use of spiritual weapons in II Corinthians 10:4, writing,

> *"For the weapon(s) of our warfare are not carnal but mighty in God for pulling down strongholds, casting down arguments and every high thing that exalts itself against the knowledge of God, bringing every thought into captivity to the obedience of Christ."*

I'm sure you've noticed my repeated use of this particular text throughout our study. This was intentional, because this verse is one of the anchor Scriptures referencing the reality of the daily war in which we find ourselves as believers. I want to slow down a bit here and unpack this all-important text, which teaches some of the most important principles and truths in the Bible regarding spiritual warfare.

Let me restate it again as it is so strongly emphasized in Scripture:

Our enemy is real!

The devil is on a mission, and he will not retreat until we confront him with everything our Heavenly Father has provided us in this battle.

The first truth I want to focus on in this text is Paul's phrase, "mighty in God." As effective and useful as our weapons may be, their power comes from God. Because of this, they are *only* mighty *in* God.

Our strength in battle comes from an intimate and personal relationship with Jesus Christ. If we are not in a right relationship with God, we have no ability—and should have no expectation—to defeat the enemy.

In the most basic terms, having saving faith and living right in response to that faith is our greatest weapon against the enemy of our souls. By committing to a lifestyle that is Scripturally based and pleasing to God, we mount a defense against all weapons the enemy wields.

Paul closes this verse saying we should be "bringing every thought into captivity to the obedience of Christ." With obedience, we punish all disobedience. The Prophets taught that God values obedience over sacrifice. Simply put, living right (by the Word of God) is our most powerful defense against the enemy. When we compromise our convictions and live contrary to the Word of God in any area of our lives, we give the enemy fuel to use against us. Living in absolute obedience to the will and Word of God robs Satan of opportunities to come against us.

In God (cultivating and maintaining an intimate relationship) is the most critical issue we face in this never-ending war.

All other weapons are connected to this. We must heed Paul's admonition regarding this in order to experience the mighty power of God through the weapons He provides.

Next, I want to reemphasize our focus and three-fold mission in this battle.

First, we must pull down every stronghold erected in our personal lives by our disobedience and the schemes of the enemy. A stronghold is anything that blocks us from the presence and provision of God. It can be an attitude or activity we've permitted to arise in our lives that is not acceptable to God. Like David, we must ask the Holy Spirit to search our hearts and minds. We must pray that God would open our eyes to sins of which we need to repent. Then we must renounce them.

"Pulling down" denotes intentional effort and work on our part. We must acknowledge that strongholds exist. Then, by submitting to God through obedience, we go about destroying them. If you think they are too big and strong to take on, you're right! But you don't fight alone. Pull out your sword of the Spirit, the Word of God, and use it against Satan. "You are of God, little children, and have overcome them, because He who is in you is greater than he who is in the world." (I John 4:4)

Second, we must address and cast down every argument and high thing that exalts itself against the knowledge of God. As previously stated, this is the battle in our minds. Satan is the author of confusion and chaos. His purpose is to rob us of God's peace and purpose in our lives.

We combat this by saturating ourselves in the presence of God through prayer, praise, and worship. Worship was never intended as just a Sunday thing. It is a powerful weapon we should utilize everyday. True worship brings us into the presence of God and binds any attempt of the enemy to defeat us. Note the exhortation of the Psalmist in Psalm 149:5–9:

> *"Let the saints be joyful in glory; let them sing aloud on their beds. Let the high praises of God be in their mouth, and a two-edged sword in their hand, to execute vengeance on the nations, and punishments on the peoples; to bind their kings with chains, and their nobles with fetters of iron; to execute on them the written judgment this honor have all the saints."*

Worship honors God and puts Him in His rightful place in our lives. It also puts the devil in his rightful place. When we focus on our Heavenly Father, it diminishes the enemy's ability to confuse and cloud our thinking. Paul understood the power of this principle. He teaches in I Thessalonians 5:18, "In everything give thanks; for this is the will of God in Christ Jesus for you."

Third, we must bring every thought into captivity to the obedience of Christ. Not only do we need to know the Word of God, but we also must apply it to our daily lives. James, the Bishop of the early church, emphasizes this truth in his writing.

> *"Therefore lay aside all filthiness and overflow of wickedness, and receive with meekness the implanted word, which is able to save your souls. But be doers of the word, and not hearers only, deceiving yourselves. For if anyone is a hearer of the word and not a doer, he is like a man observing his natural face in a mirror, for he observes himself, goes away, and immediately forgets what kind of man he was. But he who looks into the perfect law of liberty and continues in it, and is not*

a forgetful hearer but doer of the work, this one will be blessed in what he does." (James 1:21–25)

The importance of obedience cannot be overstated, especially in spiritual warfare. God has given us weapons and every good thing we need to succeed. But if we don"t live right, all these weapons are powerless. Obedience is a decision that determines our destiny.

With a clear understanding of our focus and mission in warfare, I now turn to the weapons provided for us, which are cataloged by Paul in Ephesians 6:14–18.

> *"Stand therefore, having girded your waist with truth, having put on the breastplate of righteousness, and having shod your feet with the preparation of the gospel of peace; above all, taking the shield of faith with which you will be able to quench all the fiery darts of the wicked one. And take the helmet of salvation and the sword of the Spirit, which is the Word of God, praying always with all prayer and supplication in the Spirit, being watchful to this end with all perseverance and supplication for all the saints."*

There are other weapons found in Scripture, but Paul focuses on the major ones provided by our Heavenly Father through the in-working of His Holy Spirit in our lives.

Let's unpack this arsenal and carefully examine each one in order to equip ourselves for the battles we must face. As we do this, note that the responsibility for *putting on* these weapons rests on our shoulders. God has provided them, but we must pick them up and utilize them on a daily basis. *Putting on* implies our role in applying these truths to our daily lives.

Pulling Down Strongholds

Paul begins with the importance of **standing**. We must intentionally make a decision to remain faithful in our relationship with Jesus and not compromise our convictions or lifestyle in any way. Remember, these weapons are only "mighty in God."

Once we have a firm commitment to our faith and refuse to be moved by circumstances, we are ready to pick up these weapons. First, we must take up the **battle belt** and gird our waists with **truth**. The belt holds everything in place and for believers, it is the truth of God's Word.

Every action we take must be grounded in the teachings of the Bible. In Corinthians, Paul teaches us that our weapons are not carnal but spiritual. We do not war according to our own opinions and ideas but rather by the power of God's Word. This is why we must make it a priority to get in the Word every day. Without it we cannot know the truth that sets us free.

Once we understand the truth and are grounded in it, we put on the **breastplate of righteousness**. Here again the emphasis is on obedience or right living. If we aren't committed to a lifestyle based in Biblical convictions, we will never stand against the devil and his schemes.

As previously taught, right living is a powerful weapon that renders our enemy powerless in his attempts to defeat us. The breastplate is a defensive weapon that quenches all his fiery darts and protects us from injury and destruction. We must hold firmly to it and make sure it is in its proper place in our lives at all times if we are going to win this war.

Unfortunately, many view righteousness as a lofty, unattainable concept. We would rather focus on grace. But Scripture teaches that *we are* the righteousness of God in Christ Jesus (II Corinthians 5:21). If we believe this truth, then we realize the battle to live righteously on a daily basis is not as complicated as we make it. It is a matter of relationship and decision.

We desperately need to look at our decision-making process. Every decision we make has consequences—some good, some bad. As we grow, each of us develops a personal belief system that determines the decisions we make. If our beliefs are not grounded in the Word of God, we will make decisions based on what we feel rather than our faith.

Herein lies the battle. Ask yourself: Do I do what I do because of how I think (feel) or do I make sound decisions on what I know (faith)?

The more we fill our hearts and minds with God's Word, the easier it will be to make the right decisions regardless of how we feel.

There's a psychological principle that holds up for believers and nonbelievers: "I do what I do because of how I feel; I feel the way I feel because of how I think. Therefore if I want to change how I live, I must learn how to change how I think."

Paul teaches this in many of his writings. Prayerfully study Romans 12:1–2, Philippians 4:8, II Corinthians 4:16, Ephesians 4:23, and Philippians 4:6–7. These are just a few verses that challenge us to depend on the Holy Spirit to renew our minds on a consistent basis. This can only occur when we are in a right relationship with our Heavenly Father.

Understanding the significance of the breastplate of righteousness and holding it firmly, let's continue to unpack our arsenal of weapons so that we can utilize them in battle.

Paul next teaches us to have our feet covered with the **preparation (shoes) of the Gospel of peace**. We should not find it strange that one of our primary weapons of war is peace. Peace—true peace—comes only in and through God. Paul is teaching the truth of walking in the Word of God. We can't just read and study His word. We must apply it to our lives and walk in it every day, in every circumstance.

The word *preparation* denotes our responsibility. Once again, God provides everything we need, but we must pick it up and use it. This cannot be overstated. Our feet should be completely covered with the truth of the Gospel, and we are to walk therein. There is no shortcut nor substitute.

Note what Paul taught Timothy. "Be diligent to present yourself approved to God, a worker who does not need to be ashamed, rightly dividing the word of truth." (II Timothy 2:15) Walking (living) consistently in the Word of God will not only produce peace but also victory in every area of our lives.

Our next weapon and the one Paul says is most important is the **shield of faith** with which we can quench the enemy's fiery darts. *Faith* references what we believe, with an emphasis on the Word of God and our relationship with Him.

In Romans 10:17 we are taught, "So then faith comes by hearing and hearing by the Word of God." As clearly stated, God's Word shields us from all attempts of the enemy to influence us and lead us into chaos, confusion, and defeat.

We must never lay down our shield but rather keep it close every day, in every circumstance. It is our most powerful defensive weapon in this war.

Our personal opinions cannot ward off the power of our enemy, but faith in our Savior can. Keep that faith close, polished, and ready to use every day of your life.

The fifth weapon listed is the **helmet of salvation**. It is interesting that salvation is listed as a helmet, that which protects our minds/brains. Salvation has been provided by the blood of Jesus and it is something we must accept. Salvation is not an emotional experience but a carefully thought out decision to receive God's life-changing grace and follow Jesus. Being born again brings a change in how we live and think.

As we grow in our relationship with Christ, we naturally develop our faith. And as Paul taught in Philippians 2:5, the very mind of Christ is imparted unto us in the process. This helmet is a powerful weapon that enables us to think clearly and decisively against the enemy's attempts to sidetrack and derail us.

I am concerned that many confuse a relationship with the Church and a relationship with God. Of course, the Church is important and one of God's priorities. We are His bride. But we don't receive salvation by joining a local church congregation. Our salvation comes only through the blood of Christ and our personal acceptance of His grace. I am not saved because I am in a church. I am a part of His Church because I am saved. The helmet of salvation protects me from thinking otherwise and keeps the enemy from tricking and destroying me.

Next, we are told to take the **sword of the Spirit**, which is the Word of God. This is one of our offensive weapons. Its importance is stated in Hebrews 4:12.

"For the Word of God is living and powerful, and sharper than any two-edged sword, piercing even to the division of soul and spirit, and of joints and marrow, and is a discerner of the thoughts and intents of the heart."

His Word is living and powerful. We must learn how to properly use it to discern (know) the thoughts and intents of the heart. The Word of God, rightly applied, reveals the difference between what I *think* and *feel* and what my faith dictates.

We cannot defeat the enemy without this sword of the

Spirit. That is why there is such an overwhelming emphasis placed on its importance throughout Scripture. We desperately need to saturate our hearts and minds with God's Word if we are to stand against Satan's constant attempts to conquer us. There is no more effective weapon in our arsenal than the sword of the Spirit.

Our Lord Jesus mightily used this weapon against Satan when tempted in the wilderness. Shouldn't we follow suit?

Paul concludes with reference to two weapons we should understand in our current times. These are **prayer** and **perseverance**.

We already discussed the importance of **prayer**, but it bears repeating. Believers need to understand that prayer is a defensive *and* offensive weapon. "Praying always with all prayer and supplication (in the Spirit)." (Ephesians 6:18) Prayer empowers us and enables us to see clearly what we need to know to remain victorious in our walk with God.

Perseverance speaks to our determination to never give up. As Paul wrote, "Having done all to stand, stand. . . ." In some circumstances all we can do is to stand. So we stand, believing even when we don't fully see what God is doing. We stand even though our feelings are overwhelmed and our faith seems to be depleted. We stand on His Word, believing all that He has promised even if we can't see it with our eyes.

We must make a decision to ignore Satan's lies and deception and continue believing that all things work together for our good, as promised in Romans 8:28. Remember, the battle is most often in our minds. By standing on the Word of God, we allow the Holy Spirit to renew our minds to see the victory.

I will close this section by defining our spiritual weapons with the statement of faith given by Paul in Romans 8:31–39.

"What then shall we say to these things? If God is for us, who can be against us? He who did not spare his own son, but delivered him up for us all, how shall He not with Him also freely give us (all) things? Who shall bring a charge against God's elect? It is God who justifies. Who is he who condemns? It is Christ who died, and furthermore is also risen, who is even at the right hand of God, who also makes intercession for us. Who shall separate us from the love of Christ? Shall tribulation, or distress, or persecution, or famine, or nakedness, or peril, or sword? As it is written: 'For your sake we are killed all day long; we are accounted as sheep for the slaughter.' Yet in all these we are more than conquerors through Him who loved us. For I am persuaded that neither death nor life, nor angels nor principalities nor powers, nor things present nor things to come, nor height nor depth, nor any other created thing, shall be able to separate us from the love of God which is in Christ Jesus our Lord."

This is an anchor Scripture in my life. I highly recommend meditating on it regularly it to anyone who is serious about winning this war.

EPILOGUE: LIVING VICTORIOUSLY

I n Revelation 2:7, we are given an exhortation and informa- tion regarding the reward for those who live victoriously in Christ Jesus.

"He who has an ear, let him hear what the Spirit says to the churches. To him who overcomes will I give to eat from the tree of life, which is in the midst of the paradise of God."

In this verse we are given an imperative to understand the war in which we're involved. Additionally, we're reminded of the need to live rightly so we can become the overcomers Jesus intends us to be.

In this study I have attempted to provide a practical under- standing of the fundamentals of spiritual warfare and the on- going battles we all face. It has not been my intention to bring undue attention to Satan, our enemy, but to give insight into his character and mission. I sincerely believe these truths are critically important to properly equip you to be a good soldier in God's army.

In these final pages, I will discuss our responsibility to fight in this war. Throughout our study I have spoken of living rightly as a powerful weapon that overwhelms the enemy's attempts to destroy us. Understanding who we are in Christ Jesus and the fact that He empowers us to live in righteousness by faith is basic to our victory.

Satan wants us to believe that we are weak and that it is natural to sin every day. His mission is to distract us from the truth that Jesus has given us all power and authority over Satan. By the indwelling power of the Holy Spirit, Jesus equipped us to overcome Satan's every attempt to defeat us.

Will we sin? Until this life ends, yes. But we should not be satisfied to accept our sinful nature as if we there is no hope for sanctification. Remember—the same Spirit that raised Christ from the dead is in you!

It is critical that you and I learn to walk in the Spirit so we can overcome the lust of the flesh with all of its desires. As this book comes to a close, I want to share four simple but challenging steps that we can take to accomplish this. Take these steps and you will learn how to live in victory on a daily basis.

Step 1: Cultivate right desires. Practically speaking, everything we do in life is motivated by what we desire in any given moment. The Apostle John exhorts us in I John 2: 15–17,

"Do not love the world or the things in the world. If anyone loves the world, the love of the Father is not in him. For all that is in the world—the lust of the flesh, the lust of the eyes, and the pride

of life—is not of the Father but is of the world. And the world is passing away, and the lust of it; but he who does the will of God abides forever."

This is why it is so important that we adjust our focus in life and learn how to walk in the Spirit. Note the instruction of the Apostle Paul in his letter to the church in Galatia.

"I say then: Walk in the spirit, and you shall not fulfill the lust of the flesh. For the flesh lusts against the Spirit, and the Spirit against the flesh; and these are contrary to one another, so that you do not the things that you wish. But if you are led by the Spirit, you are not under the law." (Galatians 5:16–18)

By submitting to the lordship of Jesus Christ, you allow Him to fill you with His Spirit. When this happens, He enables you to live in His power, to overcome the flesh and all that is in the world. Simply put, He changes your focus, thus changing your desires, which changes the way you live.

This is not complicated, but it is difficult. It is a daily battle in which we must intentionally apply the Word of God to our lives. James gives us the same principle in his writing. James 4:7–10 instructs us,

"Therefore submit to God. Resist the devil and he will flee from you. Draw near to God and He will draw near to you. Cleanse your hands, you sinners; and purify your hearts, you double-minded. Lament and mourn and weep! Let your laughter be turned to mourning and your joy to gloom. Humble yourselves in the sight of the Lord, and He will lift you up."

PULLING DOWN STRONGHOLDS

Humility overcomes worldliness and enables us to rightly focus on what is important in life. Cultivating and maintaining pure desires is a daily struggle. Yet, while we live in the world, we are not of this world. Therefore, our focus must remain on the things of God. Paul teaches this same principle in his letter to the Colossians. In Colossians 3: 1-4, he writes,

> *"If then you were raised with Christ, seek those things which are above, where Christ is, sitting at the right hand of God. Set your mind on things above, not on things on the earth. For you died, and your life is hidden with Christ in God. When Christ who is our life appears, then you also will appear with Him in glory."*

What we focus on determines what we desire. One of the nine fruits of the Spirit is self-control. By walking in the Spirit, this fruit is produced and helps us focus on the right things. In the end, this produces right desires. It is difficult but it can be attained if we simply adjust our focus.

Step 2: Learn to make right decisions. Every decision in life has consequences, and good decisions don't happen by accident. They're made intentionally. Unfortunately, most of us make decisions based on our feelings, and our feelings can deceive us.

There is a vast difference in reacting and responding to a situation in life. Reacting is based on emotions (feelings), while responding is based on the mind (thinking). If I make a decision in the moment based on what I feel, it is usually a bad decision. On the other hand, if I discipline myself to think before I act, I will respond based on what I know rather than what I feel.

To respond more often than I react, I rely on a tool that has proven invaluable in my life: focus statements. A focus statement is a brief question I ask myself when my emotions are taking over in a given situation. I have several focus statements that I use almost every day.

Examples include:

Why do I feel this way?

Why do I want to do what I am about to do?

If I do what I am thinking of doing, how will it affect my relationship with God, my family, and others?

I always use the last question when confronted with an important decision. Regardless of which question I turn to, the purpose is the same. Focus statements cause me to stop and think before I act.

I encourage you to adopt my focus statements or create some that work for you. The important thing is that we discipline ourselves to make decisions on what we know (our faith) rather than on what we feel in any given moment.

As you consider focus statements, remind yourself that every one of your decisions determines your destiny and the quality of your life.

In life, we all make bad decisions, some with life-changing consequences. What do we do when this happens? Let me suggest three things to help you.

First, *admit your mistake and face the consequences*, even though it may be extremely painful. Second, if at all possible, *fix it*. Humble yourself and render a sincere apology and seek forgiveness from those you have hurt. When possible, make restitution to anyone who suffered loss because of your choices. Third, *understand that some decisions can't be fixed*, regardless of how badly you feel. Not in this life. In those cases, seek God's forgiveness and allow His grace to strengthen and comfort you. Then ask

Him to help you move forward. People may not forgive you, but God will. And not only does He forgive your sins, but according to His Word, He forgets them. He puts them out of His mind. He will never hold past sins and mistakes against you if you have put them under the blood of Christ. This is a wonderful truth about our God. He forgives all our trespasses and sins. When we sincerely confess and repent, He casts our sins into a sea of forgetfulness (Psalm 103), never to remember them again.

Step 3: Live disciplined lives. Discipline (self-control) is not a popular word or concept in today's culture. We want the freedom to do whatever we want to do, whenever we want to do it. In our microwave society, we are so focused on instant gratification that we don't like being told, "No." The dominant philosophy of our times is that if it feels good, it is okay.

Despite what culture says, many things are not acceptable unto our God. To please our Heavenly Father, we must practice discipline in every area of our lives.

As previously discussed, He has provided us with the power of His Spirit to enable us to live above this world and all of its lust. However, to accomplish this we must do our part. God will not force us to conform to His will nor force us to live rightly. He has given what Scripture teaches to be *free will*. He has given us the privilege and the responsibility to choose whom we will serve, and we cannot serve both God and man (ourselves).

Living disciplined lives according to God's Word is a decision each of us must make individually. I must establish my own priorities in life and discipline myself—with His help—to live by His laws and not my own nor the standards of this world. Discipline is intentional. It comes from establishing good habits out of commitment to a lifestyle that is pleasing to God. It is a daily battle, but we can win if we stay focused on our personal mission and purpose in life.

We are here to serve and honor God. To be successful on this journey, we must establish and maintain priorities that keep us moving forward. Cultivating a personal and intimate relationship with Jesus is the key to victory in every area of life.

Step 4: Develop a mindset of determination. Remember what Paul taught in Ephesians 6:13: "Having done all to stand—stand therefore. . . ."

As previously taught, our greatest battle takes place in the mind. We have to make a decision to live by faith, not feelings. As we develop unwavering faith in the person and promises of God, circumstances cannot move us. As taught in Hebrews 12:1–2, we must fix our focus on Him who never changes.

> *"Therefore we also, since we are surrounded by so great a cloud of witnesses, let us lay aside every weight, and the sin which so easily ensnares us, and let us run with endurance the race that is set before us, looking unto Jesus, the author and finisher of our faith, who for the joy that was set before him endured the cross, despising the shame, and has sat down at the right hand on the throne of God."*

On this journey, you will encounter many obstacles and potholes. Inevitability, you will slip and fall. When this happens, focus on Jesus. Remind yourself that He is your best friend, that He has promised to walk this journey with you, that He is present to pick you up and give you the strength to keep going. We cannot find victory within ourselves. Therefore, we must learn to totally depend upon Him. As promised, He will never leave or forsake us.

Pulling Down Strongholds

Whatever you do, don't give up. You may feel inadequate and weak, but remind yourself that you are who Father says you are. You are a child of God, and no weapon formed against you can prosper (Isaiah 54:17). God not only destines you for a specific pathway, but also He has empowered you by His Spirit to finish the race in victory.

Don't fall victim to distraction and discouragement. Foster a strong mindset of determination to become the person God designed you to be. Determination will keep you moving forward and give you the strength and fortitude to successfully navigate rough places.

Remember that determination is a matter of the mind, not the body. You will grow tired and weary both physically and emotionally. There will be plenty of opportunities to quit. But determination, partnered with the Holy Spirit working in you, will keep you focused and moving forward.

In summary, let me remind you again that He has made us more than conquerors through Christ Jesus. If we seek the right desires and work to make the right decisions grounded by a disciplined life with an unshakable determination, we will not be held back by strongholds. We will live as victors over them.

THE CHURCH'S DECLARATION

Satan, listen up, listen now, listen long, and listen well. We are the Church of the living God.

We are bought with blood, charged with power, married to Jesus, indwelt with his Spirit, immune from destruction, and destined for victory!

We won't fear your foolish fables, run from your roaring, fold under your fire, be vulnerable to your vehemence, be scattered by your schemes, be derailed by your deception, be lulled by your lies, buckle under your barking, acquiesce under your attack, or be scared by your subtlety!

We're part of the company of the committed, the crowd of the covenant, the congregation of the courageous, and a crew of the commissioned. We're a fellowship of the faithful, the battalion of believers, the regiment of the redeemed, the division of the devoted, the army of the approved, the team of the triumphant, the lot of the Lord, the platoon of the powerful, and the vestige of the victorious.

We're not here to dread the war, plan the war, study the war, or discuss the war. We've come to win the war!

Satan, the clock is running out for you. We await our rapture and your rupture, our consummation and your condemnation, our reign and your ruin, our victory and your vagrancy, our success and your sorrow. You can summon all your hosts, but you lose the battle, for He that is in us is greater than he that is in the world.

We're the Church of the living God, blood-washed, Spirit-filled, battle-scarred, unrelenting, and indestructible.

THE GATES OF HELL SHALL NOT PREVAIL AGAINST US!

Made in the USA
Columbia, SC
21 December 2020

29679656R00039